Brinton W. Woodward

The Ladies' Floral Calender

and household receipt book

Brinton W. Woodward

The Ladies' Floral Calender
and household receipt book

ISBN/EAN: 9783337271978

Printed in Europe, USA, Canada, Australia, Japan

Cover: Foto ©Andreas Hilbeck / pixelio.de

More available books at **www.hansebooks.com**

GO CULL THE GOLDEN FRUITS OF TRUTH ;
GO GATHER FANCY'S BRILLIANT FLOWERS.

THE LADIES'

FLORAL CALENDAR,

AND

HOUSEHOLD

RECEIPT BOOK.

PUBLISHED BY

B. W. WOODWARD,

LAWRENCE, KANSAS.

LAWRENCE REPUBLICAN BOOK AND JOB OFFICE.

In the hope that it will find its appropriate place in the sphere of pleasant entertainment, as well as of practical utility, we commend this little book to a discriminating public. The Calendars are arranged for convenience of reference, and are good for two years—1869 and 1870. The "Dial of Flowers"—probably a new idea to most of our readers, will be found pleasing and suggestive. The "Floral Languages" are correctly collated from standard authorities on those "voiceless tongues;" whilst the selections of poetry will, we think, be found both choice and appropriate.

The cooking receipts found herein are all *practical*. Whilst any housekeeper can follow them, and "set a table good enough for a king," the materials prescribed are neither rare nor expensive, but within the reach of ordinary households. Every one has been thoroughly tested before including it in the selection.

Preserve this little book. New editions will be published from time to time, with fresh selections and valuable new receipts.

◆ ◆ ◆

The following, from E. B. Hamlin, of the Collier Lead Co., St. Louis, universally known in the Drug and Paint Trade of the West, needs no comment from us.

ST. LOUIS, Mo., May 16th, 1868.

B. W. WOODWARD, Lawrence, Kansas:

Dear Sir: While on a visit to your city, in March last, I was suffering from a severe attack of Chills and Fever, and, with my system prostrated from the effects of the Typhoid Fever, from which I had but recently convalesced, I was in a very bad condition of health. I procured a bottle each of your "Ague Cure" and "Elixir of Calisaya Bark and Iron," and almost from the moment I began their use, I experienced a relief from the disagreeable symptoms attending the disease, and within a week thereafter was entirely rid of them. I continued their use until the contents of each bottle were consumed, when I found myself in possession of more than my usual vigor, and since that time have been in the enjoyment of better health than I have for several years past. Because of their prompt and happy effects in my case, I deem it but justice to yourself and your remedies to make an acknowledgement of the same; and you are at liberty to make such use of this as you may deem proper.

With highest regards, I remain,

Yours very truly,   E. B. HAMLIN.

```
    1  2  3  4            1  2     1  2  3  4  5  6              1  2  3  4
 6  7  8  9 10 11     3  4  5  6  7  8  9     7  8  9 10 11 12 13    5  6  7  8  9 10 11
13 14 15 16 17 18    10 11 12 13 14 15 16    14 15 16 17 18 19 20   12 13 14 15 16 17 18
20 21 22 23 24 25    17 18 19 20 21 22 23    21 22 23 24 25 26 27   19 20 21 22 23 24 25
27 28 29 30          24 25 26 27 28 29 30    28 29 30              26 27 28 29 30 31
                     31
```

CALENDAR FOR 1870.

JANUARY.							FEBRUARY.							MARCH.							APRIL.						
M	T	W	T	F	S	S	S	M	T	W	T	F	S	S	M	T	W	T	F	S	S	M	T	W	T	F	S
						1			1	2	3	4	5			1	2	3	4	5						1	2
3	4	5	6	7	8	9	6	7	8	9	10	11	12	6	7	8	9	10	11	12	3	4	5	6	7	8	9
10	11	12	13	14	15	16	13	14	15	16	17	18	19	13	14	15	16	17	18	19	10	11	12	13	14	15	16
17	18	19	20	21	22	23	20	21	22	23	24	25	26	20	21	22	23	24	25	26	17	18	19	20	21	22	23
24	25	26	27	28	29	30	27	28						27	28	29	30	31			24	25	26	27	28	29	30
31																											

MAY							JUNE							JULY.							AUGUST.						
1	2	3	4	5	6	7			1	2	3	4						1	2	1	2	3	4	5	6		
8	9	10	11	12	13	14	5	6	7	8	9	10	11	3	4	5	6	7	8	9	7	8	9	10	11	12	13
15	16	17	18	19	20	21	12	13	14	15	16	17	18	10	11	12	13	14	15	16	14	15	16	17	18	19	20
22	23	24	25	26	27	28	19	20	21	22	23	24	25	17	18	19	20	21	22	23	21	22	23	24	25	26	27
29	30	31					26	27	28	29	30			24	25	26	27	28	29	30	28	29	30	31			
														31													

SEPTEMBER   OCTOBER.   NOVEMBER.   DECEMBER.

WOODWARD'S
STANDARD PREPARATIONS

Medicinal, or for the Toilet.

WOODWARD'S AGUE CURE,
For Fever and Ague, Dumb Ague and Bilious Fevers.

BLOOD AND LIVER RENOVATOR,
For all diseases arising from impurity of the Blood or inactivity of the Liver.

COMPOUND AROMATIC BLACKBERRY SYRUP,
For Diarrhœa, Dysentery, Colic, &c., &c.

GERMANIA HAIR RENEWER,
To promote the Growth and restore the Life and Color of the Hair.

ELIXIR CALISAYA AROMATIC,
An invaluable Tonic and Stimulant and Preventive of Chills and Fever.

ELIXIR CALISAYA BARK AND IRON,
A Restorative for all Nervous and Debilitated Conditions of the System.

KANSAS EYE BALM,
For Diseases of the Eye, Acute or Chronic.

SAPONACEOUS TOOTH POWDER,
An agreeable Dentrifice, to preserve and beautify the Teeth.

FRAGRANT OIL OF SUNFLOWERS,
An unequalled Dressing for the Hair.

CRYSTAL GLYCERINE SOAP
Softens and purifies the Skin, removes Tan and Sunburn, and prevents Chapping.

SOLUTION OF CITRATE MAGNESIA,
A most delightful Aperient and cooling Purgative.

The attention of the Trade and the Public is solicited to the special preparations enumerated in the above list. Those for the Toilet are among the most elegant and beneficial of their class ever put upon the market, whilst they are put at prices below those of any approaching them in quality. The Medicinal preparations are not heralded as absolute "cure-alls," but are the result of careful study, experiment and combinations of the best remedies known to science for the prevention and cure of Disease. They are likewise t'. most *agreeable preparations of their respective kinds in the market.* Their flavor is unobjectionable; and yet their *efficiency* is unexcelled, whilst, as *safe* family Medicines, they are guaranteed, and should therefore find a place in every household.

DIAL OF FLOWERS.

"Shall I sing of happy hours,
Numbered by opening and closing flowers?"

TIME OF OPENING.

	MORNING.	
	H.	M
Yellow Goat's Beard.	3	5
Late Flowering Dandelion	4	0
Wild Succory	4	5
Naked-stalked Poppy.	5	0
Copper Colored Day Lily	5	0
Convolvulus	5	6
Common Dandelion	5	6
Spotted Achyrophorus	6	7
White Water Lily	7	0
Garden Lettuce	7	0
African Marigold	7	0
Common Pimpernel.	7	8
Mouse Ear Hawkweed.	8	0
Proliferous Pink	8	0
Field Marygold	9	0
Portulacca.	9	10
Creeping Mallow	9	10
Chickweed	9	10

CLOSING.

"Oh! let us live, so that flower by flower,
Shutting in turn, may leave
A lingerer still for the sunset hour.
A charm for the shaded eve."

	H	*M.
Late Flowering Dandelion	12	0
Creeping Mallow	12	1
Proliferous Pink	1	0
Mouse Ear Hawkweed	2	0
Common Pimpernel	2	3
Field Marigold	3	0
African Marigold	3	4
Convolvulus	4	5
Spotted Achyrophorus	4	5
White Water Lily	5	0
Naked-stalked Poppy.	7	0
Copper Colored Day Lily	7	8
Wild Succory	8	9
Common Dandelion	8	9
Yellow Goat's Beard.	9	10
Chickweed	9	10
Garden Lettuce	10	0
Portulacca	11	12

*The time here stated is from noon to night

Rose, Ivy, Myrtle—*To Beauty, Friendship and Love.*

Oh, Beauty! bright Rose of the world,
Oh, Love! the soul's Myrtle for ever,
Oh, Friendship! fair vine round a breaking heart curled
Without whose soft bonds it would sever!
For you a rich garland we braid,
Breathing sighs of pure incense above;
It will bloom in the sun, it will smile in the shade,
For Beauty, for Friendship and Love!

MRS. OSGOOD.

Wherever Woodward's Floral Calender and Receipt Book is distributed all of Woodward's Standard Family Medicines will be found for sale at some store in the vicinity, and especially by all Druggists and dealers who circulate, gratuitously, this valuable little book. Woodward's celebrated medicines are *the best* in quality, and the prices of them all are so reasonable as to place them within the reach of all.

There's wit in every flower if you can gather it.—SHIRLEY.

Bluebottle Centaury—*Delicacy.*

Her love is pure, and glad, and true,
As yonder heaven of stainless blue.

MRS. OSGOOD.

We have given the Glycerine Soap manufactured at Dr. B. W. Woodward's drug house a thorough trial, and can honestly recommend it as being the best washing compound we have ever tried. It possesses great cleansing qualities, and leaves the skin soft and smooth. In addition to being of the best quality, it is sold at an extremely low price.—*Lawrence Daily Tribune.*

Its sides I'll plant with dew sweet eglantine
And honeysuckle, full of clear bee wine.

KEATS.

We have long known Dr. B. W. Woodward as a skillful, experienced and successful Pharmaceutist. His special preparations command an extensive sale, and enjoy a high reputation throughout our State.

E. G. ROSS, U. S. Senator from Kansas.
SIDNEY CLARKE, M. C.   "

Washington, D. C., May 7, 1867.

There's a bliss beyond all that the minstrel has told,
When two that are linked in one heavenly tie,
With heart never changing and brow never cold,
Love on through all ills, and love on till they die.

Moore.

LANGUAGE OF FLOWERS.

FLOWER	SENTIMENT.
American Cowslip	My only hope.
Arbor Vitæ	Unchanging friendship.
Apple Blossom	My preference.
African Marigold	Vulgarity.
Alyssum, Sweet	Worth above Beauty.
Almond	Carelessness.
American Starwort	I bid you welcome.
Aconite	Expectation.
Aster, China	Sorrow.
Azalea	Romance.
Balm	Sympathy.
Balsam	Impatience.
Blue Centaury, Bell	Fidelity.
Bluebell	Delicacy.
Pea	No sensitive.
Bachelor's Button	Hope.
Bell flower	Ingratitude.
Camelia	Pity.
Geranium, Tall	Indifference.
Carnation, Yellow	Disdain.
Crocus	Happiness.
Cherry Blossom	Educated
China	Variety.
China, Pink	Aversion.
Geranium, uneta	I love.
Geranium	Artifice.
Clover, is	Industry.
Cockscomb	Foppery.
Columbine	Folly.
Convolvulus	Dead hope.
Cowslip	Thoughtlessness.
Cypress	Mourning.
Coreopsis	Love at first sight.
Dahlia	Fickleness.
Dandelion	Coquetry.
Daisy	Innocence.
Daffodil	Delusion.
Dead Leaves	Heavy heart.
Dogwood, Flowering	Am I indifferent to You?
Evergreen	Poverty.
Eglantine	Poetry.
Evening Primrose	Can't trust You.

"Full many a gem of purest ray serene
The dark unfathomed caves of ocean bear,
Full many a flower is born to blush unseen
And waste its sweetness on the desert air."

The countless myriads of gorgeous sunflowers, blooming on the remoter Kansas prairies, suggested the utilizing of their valuable oily properties for a luxurious hair dressing; hence the origin of Woodward's Fragrant Oil of Sunflowers.

Woodbine. Honeysuckle.—*Bond of Love*.

Fragile but sweet is the woodbine wild,
Clinging wherever its beauty may rest,
Fair as the woodbine, as trusting and mild,
Oh! be thy home upon love's fond breast.

Mrs. Osgood.

Woodward's Saponaceous Tooth Powder not only thoroughly cleanses the teeth but also possesses a valuable *embalming* or *antiseptic* property, and a delicate aromatic fragrance, which makes it really a toilet luxury, as it removes all disagreeable odors, even that of tobacco, and keeps the mouth fresh and agreeable.

Gillyflower.—*Lasting Beauty*.

A thing of beauty is a joy forever;
Its loveliness increases—it will never
Pass into nothingness; but still will keep
A bower quiet for us, and a sleep
Full of sweet dreams and health.

Keats.

"Time at last sets all things even." The worthless and injurious alcoholic preparations for the hair—Ambrosias, Anbolines, &c.—have had their brief day of popularity, and now echo answers, "where are they?" The public having thoroughly tested them, have pronounced them worthless, and turned to the use of that sterling preparation, "Germania Hair Renewer," which not only supplies the place of a hair dressing, but likewise prevents the hair from falling off, and restores it, when prematurely blanched, back to its original color. Hundreds of certificates attest this. Buy a bottle and try it.

Periwinkle.—*Sweet Remembrance*.

Through primrose tufts in that sweet bower
The periwinkle trails its leaves,
And, 'tis my faith that every flower
Enjoys the air that breathes.

Wordsworth.

Woodward's Crystal Glycerine Soap is at once the most pleasant to the senses and healthful to the skin of any emollient in use, being compounded with glycerine and purified by spirit to transparency. It is richly perfumed, prevents chapping in cold weather, removes roughness, tan and sunburn, and leaves the skin soft and velvety.

FLOWERS ARE LOVE'S TRUEST LANGUAGE.

FLOWERS.	SENTIMENT.
Forget-Me-Not	True Love.
Foxglove	Insincerity.
Fuchsia	Taste.
Geranium	Lost hope.
Gilly Flower	Lasting beauty.
Grass	Usefulness.
Golden Rod	Encouragement
Hawthorn	Hope
Hazel	Reconciliation.
Heart's Ease	Think of Me.
Heliotrope.	You are loved.
Hollyhock.	Plenty.
Honeysuckle	I dream of thee.
Hop.	Dishonesty.
Hyacinth	Grief.
Ice Plant	Your looks freeze me.
Jessamine	Amiability.
Japonica	Modest worth.
Juniper	I ask protection.
Jonquil	I desire a return of affection.
Judas Tree	Betrayed.
Larkspur	Changeable.
Laurel	Glory.
Locust	Undying affection.
Lantana	Rigor.
Love-in-a-Mist.	You are a puzzle.
Linden Tree.	Marriage.
Lilac	First emotion of love.
Love-lies-bleeding	Hopeless, not heartless.
Lily	Innocence—Virtue.
Lily of the Valley	Happy again.
Magnolia	Peerless and proud.
Marigold	I'm jealous.
Mouse Ear.	Forget me not.
Mignonette .	Good, but plain.
Moss	I love children.
Mountain Pink	Lofty aspirations.
Myrtle	Unalloyed affection.
Mistletoe	I surmount all difficulties.
Nettle	Slander.
Oleander	Beware.
Olive	Peace.
Orange Flower	Chastity.
Pansy	Think of me.
Pea	Meet me by moonlight.

SEEK TO BE GOOD, BUT AIM NOT TO BE GREAT.

Sunflower.—*Smile on me still.*

The Helianthus constantly turns toward the Sun. In Peru, the "Virgins of the Sun" wore an imitation of this flower, wrought in gold.

"Eagle of Flowers! I see thee stand.
And in the Sun's noon glory gaze,
With eye like his! thy lips expand,
And fringe their disc with golden rays.
                                        Jas. Montgomery

Oh! the heart that has truly loved never forgets,
But as truly loves on to the close,
As the sunflower turns on her god when he sets
The same look that she turned when he rose.
                                        Tom. Moore

Woodward's Fragrant Oil of Sunflowers,

FOR THE HAIR.

It being universally agreed among Physiologists that, for the purposes of a Hair Dressing, *vegetable* oils are cooling and healthful whilst *fatty or animal* oils are heating and injurious to the head, perfumers have been seeking, across sea and land, that vegetable oil which should be most suitable and agreeable for the purpose, but

"We look too high for things close by:"

and it is not necessary to go the South Sea Islands for Palm or Cocoa Nut Oil, when in our own fair land, and over all the wide prairies of the Far West, grows indigenously "The Flower of the Sun." "FRAGRANT OIL OF SUNFLOWERS," as properly deodorized and richly perfumed, is the *ne plus ultra* of toilet elegance as a dressing for the Hair

Violet.—*Modesty*

Let nature spread her loveliest.
By spring or summer nurst,
Yet still I love the violet best.
Because I loved it first.

From the Lawrence Tribune, May 9th, 1867

The success of Mr. Woodward's preparations is not an accident; its secret is not alone that they are preferred as Western productions, but they have superior merit—they are not imitations, but scientifically compounded originations—the result of careful study and research. No expense is spared in their composition, and they are put up in the finest style. They are not crudely and hastily thrown upon the market—prime excellence, and not number of preparations, being his main object.

FLOWERS	SENTIMENT.
Petunia	Less proud than they deem thee
Peach blossom	My heart is thine.
Passion Flower	..Religious fervor
Phlox	Our souls are united.
Primrose, evening.	Inconstancy.
Pink, Red.	. Woman's love.
Poppy	Consolation of sleep.
Plum Tree	Keep your promises
Pennyroyal	Go away
Rose	Beauty.
Rose, Yellow	I can't trust you.
Rose-bud	My heart knows no love
Rose Geranium	You are preferred
Rose Tea	Always lovely
Rose, Wild	Simplicity.
Snapdragon	Presumption.
Snowball.	Thoughts of heaven.
Strawberry.	Perfection.
Sweetbrier	You are poetic.
Sweet William	Let this be our last
Star of Bethlehem	Reconciliation.
Ten-weeks Stock.	...Promptitude.
Sunflower	Smile on me still.
Tuberose	Dangerous pleasure.
Tulip	Declare your love.
Trumpet Flower	Let us part friends.
Tiger Lily	May thy pride defend thee.
Venus' Looking Glass	You are a flatterer.
Verbena	You are too sensitive
Violet, Blue	Love.
Violet, White.	.. Modesty.
Water Lily	You are a good talker.
Wormwood	. Absent, but not forgotten
Weeping Willow	Forsaken.
Woodbine.	Fraternal love
White Lily	Purity
Wood Sorrel.	Joy.
Yellow Lily	You are a coquette
Zinnia.	Absent friends.

THE USE OF FLOWERS.

To whisper hope, to comfort man whene'er his faith is dim;
For whoso careth for the flowers will much more care for him.

Mary Howitt.

THE BRAVEST ARE THE TENDEREST...THE LOVING ARE THE DARING.

THE WORST OF SLAVES IS HE WHOM PASSION RULES.

HOUSEHOLD RECEIPTS.

BREAKFAST AND TEA CAKES.

Soda Cakes.

Three pints of flour, one of sour milk, table-spoonful of lard, one tea-spoonful of soda and three of cream tartar, a little salt—mix the lard, cream tartar and salt, in with the flour—dissolve the soda in the milk—mix all together in a soft dough, roll out and cut—bake in a quick oven.

Corn Bread.

One quart of sour milk, one table-spoonful of soda, four ounces of butter, three table-spoonfuls of flour, three eggs, and corn meal enough to make a stiff batter.

(From Hon. F. M. Conway, formerly M. C., now U. S. Consul at Marseilles, France.)

I have been in the use of WOODWARD'S AGUE CURE for some two years past and find it to be a most admirable medicine for all bilious derangements. It is said by the proprietor to contain no mercury or other noxious substance; which if true, (and I have no reason to doubt it,) ought to secure for it a place in the household of every family.

I have found it in my experience far more efficacious than the usual remedies of blue-mass and quinine. I take it for every description of bilious affection. It is equally potent to cure fully developed chills and fever as to correct the slighter disorders of the system which are so prevalent in bilious districts in the summer and fall seasons, and which are premonitory of approaching diseases. I cheerfully recommend this medicine to all who are suffering from a deranged Liver—satisfied that whoever buys and takes it will find it a good investment.

M. F. CONWAY.

Graham Bread.

One quart of water, one cup of molasses, one cup of yeast, half a tea-spoonful of soda, one teaspoonful of sugar—pour the yeast upon the soda and let it foam, mix about as stiff as gingerbread.

Bread and Milk Pancakes.

Soak bread in the milk, and mix until perfectly smooth, then stir in flour until middling thick, raise with yeast, when light add a small piece of butter and two or three eggs, a little soda.

WOODWARD's Aromatic Blackberry Syrup is the best and pleasantest combination extant for the cure of diarrhea, dysentery, and all bowel affections. It is likewise far superior to all "soothing syrups" and other "paregoricky" mixtures for relieving the troubles of children during teething—correcting the stomach and healthily regulating the action of the bowels. It contains the concentrated extract of the blackberry, preserved in pure French brandy; combined with wholesome vegetable astringents and tonics to the bowels.

Mush Cakes.

Make about a quart of Indian meal mush—while hot add a piece of butter about the size of an egg—thin it with milk, adding a little salt, then add some flour, thin it with a teacup of yeast, then add as much more flour as will make it the consistence of dough—knead it well, set it to rise, when light, roll out, cut in round cakes, and bake on the griddle.

Of all the preparations for the Hair, such as "Restoratives," "Ambolines," " Ambrosias," &c., not one has so entirely and satisfactory met the approbation of the public as the new and wonderful

Germania Hair Renewer.

Wonderful, because it produces wonderful effects upon the diseased scalp and GRAY HAIR, curing the former and restoring the color of the latter

Being well aware that the public have been imposed upon by the many preparations which flood the market and which are very injurious both to the hair and skin we should not venture to introduce this article were it not unlike anything that has preceded it, in that it CONTAINS NO SUGAR OF LEAD, NITRATE OF SILVER, LIME, or anything in the least injurious to to the hair or skin. On the contrary each and every ingredient tends to

Promote the Growth, Restore the Life and Beauty of the Hair

AND CREATE A HEALTHY CONDITION OF THE SCALP.

By long research we are enabled to offer to the public a VEGETABLE COMPOUND that we will

Warranted to Restore Gray Hair

To its original color, whether Black, Brown or Auburn; to prevent the hair from falling off; to cause the hair to grow on bald heads where the roots are not dead; to cure the most inveterate humor of the scalp; to eradicate dandruff, and to keep the hair soft and glossy.

As a Restorer and Dressing it is unequalled by any other Hair preparation in the world, and, after a thorough trial, if it fails to do as represented, the money will be refunded.

Premium Corn Bread.

To two quarts of meal, add one pint of bread sponge, water sufficient to wet the whole, add 1 half pint of flour, and a table-spoonful of salt, let it rise, then knead well for the second time and place the dough in the oven, allow it to bake an hour and a half.

Kindness by secret sympathy is tied,
For noble souls by nature are allied.
Dryden.

Rye Drops.

One quart of buttermilk, with enough soda to sweeten it, (or sweet milk without the soda) salt, and three eggs—then thicken with rye flour, enough to drop from a spoon—butter your pans, and drop a spoonful in a place, bake half an hour, and eat warm for tea, with butter.

Rye and Indian Bread.

To two quarts of meal put one quart of rye, add salt, and two table-spoons of brown sugar, and one tea-cup of yeast—mix with water and mould it up, and put it in the pans you are to bake it in, let it get light and bake two hours.

A HEALTHFUL, invigorating tonic, that should commend itself as a proper one to the medical profession, and be free from the objection of pandering to depraved appetite for whiskey stimulants, under the specious name of "tonic bitters," has long been needed by the public. The "Elixir Calisaya Bark and Iron," as prepared by B. W. Woodward, Druggist and Manufacturing Pharmaceutist, is such a tonic free from all objections. It is no secret "patent" preparation, its formula being well known to the medical profession, and indorsed by our best physicians. After protracted fevers—for the weak stomach and loss of appetite—in those conditions of the system where the pallid cheek indicates the loss of iron from the blood—in states of nervous prostration and physical debility, its use is indicated, and will be found of invaluable benefit.

Muffins.

One quart of sweet milk, three eggs, a lump of butter the size of an egg, yeast sufficient to raise them—mix thicker than pancakes.

PICKLES.

Chow-Chow.

Eight quarts of sliced tomatoes and one quart of sliced onions, with one cup of salt—let it stand over night, then add one pound of sugar, one ounce of pepper, same of ginger, allspice, and whole cloves, one quarter pound of mustard seed, and one table-spoon of ground mustard, cover the whole with vinegar, and cook two hours.

Josh Billings remarks: "After a man has rode fast onst he never wants to go slow agin," and in like manner, any one that has once used "Woodward's Blood and Liver Renovator," and experienced its beneficial effects in correcting the secretions will never again use one of the quart bottles of "dope," formerly sold under the name of Blood Purifiers.

What is so rare as a day in June,
Then if ever come perfect days.
Lowell

Tomato Sauce.

Take one peck of green tomatoes, cut them into slices, and on every layer of tomatoes sprinkle a little salt; let it stand twenty-four hours, then take out the tomatoes; have ready six large onions, pared and sliced, and six green peppers, sliced; place in a stone jar a layer of tomatoes, a layer of onions, and a layer of pepper, with a little spice for every separate layer. The quantity of spice requisite for the above, is a half ounce of cloves, and the same of allspice and mace. Cover it with cider vinegar, and stand the jar on the stove twenty-four hours to simmer; but do not let it come to a boil. The above makes an excellent sauce for winter.

Composition Pickle.

Half a peck of green tomatoes, six onions, six green peppers, one large head of cabbage, half a pound of white mustard, half ounce of ground mace, and the same of cloves and allspice, four tablespoons of salt: chop fine, put in a kettle, and cover with cold vinegar, and boil two hours: add two tablespoons of sugar.

Sophia's Catsup.

Boil half a peck of tomatoes until they are soft, squeeze them through a fine wire sieve, and add a pint of vinegar, half a pint of salt, half ounce of cloves, same of allspice, half a tablespoon of black pepper; mix these together and boil about three hours; then bottle without straining

There is rest for the weary —there is rest for you.

Weary mother—almost worn out with anxious watching and care for your child, undergoing the ordeal of teething and the derangements of the system consequent thereon—use one bottle of that pleasant "Aromatic Blackberry Syrup," (Woodward's). Its effect on the little sufferer shall be like magic—reducing all inflammation and quieting all pain—and you may "wrap the drapery of your couch about you, and lie down to pleasant dreams.

Cole Slaw.

Chop the cabbage fine, and put it in the dish, with salt and pepper through; then heat vinegar enough to cover it, with a little butter, sugar and mustard, and one egg; stir it constantly until it comes to a boil and thicken a little; pour over the cabbage, and cover up tight.

Playford Bros., druggists, Burlingame, Kansas, say: "Woodward's Ague Cure is *the standard* ague medicine in our trade, and gives the best satisfaction of any."

Woodward's Ague Cure is a certain, speedy and safe cure for Fever and Ague, Dumb Ague, Bilious Fever, and all diseases originating in Biliary Derangement, caused by malaria.

Peach Pickles.

Take one gallon of good vinegar, and add to it four pounds of brown sugar; boil this for a few minutes, and skim off the scum that may rise; then take clingstone peaches that are fully ripe, rub them with a flannel cloth, to remove the down upon them, and stick three or four cloves in each; put them in a glass or earthen jar, and pour the liquor upon them boiling hot; cover them up, and let them stand in a cool place for a week or ten days; then pour off the liquor, and boil as before, after which return it, boiling hot, to the peaches, which should be carefully covered up and stowed away for future use.

Woodward's Ague Cure contains nothing injurious to the system; hence it may be given under any circumstances and to the most delicate.

To Pickle Plums.

Take seven pounds of fruit, one ounce of cloves, one and a half of cinnamon; put all in a jar in alternate layers of fruit and spice; to one quart of vinegar allow four pounds of brown sugar; boil it, and pour it over the fruit two successive days; the third day scald the vinegar and fruit together.

Being anxious to restore my gray hair to its original color, I tried two bottles of Wood's Hair Restorative and two of Mrs. Allen's Zylobalsam, but without any satisfactory result. I found even that my old preparation of sugar of lead and lac sulphur would do as well as either, but wouldn't put my hair back to its original color. At last I was induced to try a bottle of the Germania Hair Renewer, and to my perfect surprise and gratification my hair changed readily to its former color, and to-day it is as glossy as ever. But what was still better, it entirely relieved my head-ache, to which I had been for a long time subject.

I take great pleasure in recommending it to the public

MRS. J. D. FARREN

To Pickle Cherries

To eight pounds of fruit, take four pounds of sugar, half ounce of cloves, same of cinnamon, one quart of vinegar; boil the syrup four times and pour over the fruit; the fourth morning boil all together fifteen or twenty minutes, then take the fruit out and boil the syrup a few minutes, and pour over it

Dr. Woodward is sole proprietor and manufacturer of some of the very best remedies extant.—*Burlington Patriot*

Woodward's Germania Hair Renewer promotes the life and growth of the Hair, and restores gray hair to its original color.

Solution of Citrate of Magnesia is a delightful Refrigerant, Laxative and Purgative.

Pickled Cabbage.

Shred the cabbage, then put in a jar a layer of cabbage, and a layer of spice; take vinegar enough to cover the cabbage, with a little sugar, heat to boiling point, and pour over. Good in a week or ten days.

Pickled Onions.

Take small onions, skin them and put them in salt and water over night, then lay them in a jar and pour hot spiced vinegar over them.

Pickled Tomatoes

Take hard ripe tomatoes and skin them, put a layer of them in a jar, cover with a layer of sliced onions, horseradish, cinnamon and cloves, then a layer of tomatoes, and so on until the jar is full; cover the whole with good vinegar—cold. Ready in about two weeks

OFFICE OF DAILY AND WEEKLY COMMERCIAL,
LEAVENWORTH, June 8th, 1867.

B. W. Woodward, *Esq.*, *once*:

DEAR SIR: We have taken half a dozen of your "Hair Renewer" for our personal use, and have tried and found it an excellent article. Send it by M. C. Ls. r. We shall be happy to assist in extending its sale here in any way.

Respectfully yours. **PRESCOTT & HUME, Publishers.**

Collily.

Quarter peck of green tomatoes, same of string beans, six onions, same three cabbages, half dozen ears of corn, three carrots, and two heads of cabbage, cut them in pieces, and pack them in salt for one hour, slice the tomatoes and peppers; cut the cabbage, corn and beans; squeeze the tomatoes dry them, mix all together; add half a quarter pound each of black mustard seed, same of yellow ground mustard, one teaspoon of turmeric; cover all with vinegar, and boil slowly until tender; put in as much sweet oil as you like, just as you take off.

I certify to the beneficial effect of the Germania Hair Renewer, prepared by Dr. Woodward, in a number of cases, which was, in every case, to completely restore the original color of the hair, and to leave it soft and glossy. **ALBERT NEWMAN, M.D.**

Spiced Peaches.

Ten pounds of peaches, pared and packed into a jar, four pounds of sugar to one quart of vinegar, boiled fifteen minutes; one ounce of cloves, half ounce of mace, two ounces of cinnamon; add the spice after the vinegar has boiled fifteen minutes, then boil all five minutes longer; then pour over the peaches boiling hot, let it cool twice, each time putting it on boiling hot again; if it appears to sour, boil it again.

DESSERTS.

Apple Meringue.

Pare, core and stew ten tart apples in a very little water; add sugar, lemon, &c., as it for a pie, and put it into a fruit pie-dish, in a cool oven; beat up the whites of four eggs to a strong froth, and pile it over the apples, avoiding the edges of the dish; return it to a warm oven, and brown very slightly. Serve with cream A custard made of the yolks, and flavored with essence of vanilla, and poured over. is very nice if you have not cream.

From Hon. W. W. H. Lawrence, formerly Secretary of the State of Kansas.

During the summer and fall of 1859 I was troubled with Ague and Fever in its most *horrid forms.* For months this disease lingered about me, assuming almost every shape, both regular and irregular, common and uncommon. To arrest it I made use of the common remedy—*quinine*—in a most faithful manner, but to no effect. I also used, diligently, numerous other medicines, said to be "Ague Cures " In fact I tried almost everything I could think or hear of, but all to no purpose. And as a "dernier resort" I sent to B. W. Woodward, of Lawrence, for a package of his AGUE CURE, and it is but justice to him, and the medicine he sent me, to say that since I commenced taking it I have had but one very slight chill, and that was the next day after I got the medicine. I used one bottle Ague Cure and part of another, and a bottle of his Tonic. My health improved rapidly, and to-day I am enjoying better health than before for years.

I therefore cheerfully recommend both the Pills and Elixir as a sure and safe Ague Remedy.

Blackberry Pudding.

Take one quart of milk, add to It half a pint of sweet cream, eight eggs, eight tablespoons of flour, and one quart of blackberries; bake one hour in a quick oven. For sauce, cream the butter and sugar, cinnamon to taste

" Why will ye doubting stand.
Why still delay,"

When a little judicious assistance, now rendered to nature, will tide you over the critical time, and probably save you from a severe spell of sickness and a long doctor's bill If the liver is torpid—if you have sick headache and nausea—if you are "bilious" or have bilious diarrhœa, with occasional prolonged costiveness, don't disregard these unmistakable symptoms, nor delay any longer—for "delays are dangerous." Get a bottle of "Woodward's Blood and Liver Renovator."

Woodward's Ague Cure.—This invaluable remedy has now been in use in the West for the past ten years, and has proved its superiority over all other remedies of its class.

California Cake

Two cups of sugar, one of butter, and one of water—two eggs, three cups of flour, one teaspoon of soda, and two of cream tartar

Good common cake.

Take two cups of light bread dough, two eggs, one cup of sugar, one cup of raisins, half a cup of butter, one nutmeg, one teaspoonful of saleratus—mix them thoroughly and add a little flour; let it stand half an hour before baking

White Cake.

One teacup of sugar, butter the size of an egg—beat together—half a teaspoonful of soda put into half a cup of sweet milk, one cup of flour, one teaspoon cream tartar put into the flour, whites of four eggs—which add last of all

Fruit Cake.

One pound of butter, one of sugar, and one of flour, nine eggs, two pounds of raisins, one of currants, quarter pound of citron, wineglass of brandy, one nutmeg, tablespoonful of cinnamon, cloves.

STRUCK! FOR LESS HOURS OF WORK AND HIGHER WAGES.—How often have we seen announcements of this kind, and most of us know something of the derangements of the business industries and interests of life consequent thereon. But how often "a strike" occurs among the members of our own bodies and we are unaware of the fact, though painfully conscious of its disastrous effects. For instance: THE STOMACH has "struck"—we have overcrowded him with work every day or kept him at work until late in the night, and now he has rebelled and will work for us no longer until we give him good re t fair treatment and fee him with a bottle of "Elixir Calisaya Bark and Iron." Or, perhaps it is "that noblest Roman (and workman) of them all," THE LIVER, that has "stopped off" work, and by remaining torpid, has deranged the whole economy of the system until we give h'm an advance of a bottle of "Woodward's Blood and Liver Renovator" to stimulate up to renewed healthful activity. Treat all the members fairly and give them aid in time—so shall they not "stop off for good and all."

Mrs. R.'s Cup Cake.

One cup of sugar, half cup of butter, two eggs, half cup of milk, half teaspoon soda, teaspoon of cream tartar, one and a half cups flour, a little salt and nutmeg.

Ginger Crackers.

One cup each of sugar, molasses and shortening, one tablespoon of ginger and a little salt, one tablespoon of soda dissolved in four of vinegar or water—put the sugar, molasses, and shortening on to boil a few minutes, take off and stir in the soda, then flour enough to make them stiff, knead them, rolling thin, and bake quickly

Nice Gingerbread.

To twenty tablespoonsful of molasses and same of melted lard, are added seven teaspoons of soda dissolved in eight tablespoons of boiling water, two tablespoons of crushed alum dissolved in three tablespoons of boiling water, one tablespoon of ginger, and a little salt if the lard is fresh—the whole well stirred together. Then four tablespoons of cream of tartar are mixed thoroughly with a pint or so of flour, and stirred in gently with enough more flour added to make a dough as soft as it can be conveniently rolled; bake in a quick oven.

Demmie's Premium Sponge Cake.

Six eggs, the weight of five of them in sugar, and three of flour—beat the whites and yolks separately very light, then put them together and beat again, put in the sugar by degrees, beating hard all the time, and lastly stir in the flour very gently, by degrees—flavor to suit the taste. The above is reliable.

WARRENSBURG, MISSOURI, MAY 3D, 1866.

DR. WOODWARD:

Sir—Two months ago, I received a bottle of the "Germania Hair Renewer" from you, and since that time I have been using it as directed. At the time I commenced using it my hair was fast falling off, but it soon stopped, and I have reason to believe it was owing to the use of the "Renewer." It has not altogether restored it to its natural color, but it has certainly improved it greatly, and I have not yet used more than one-half of the bottle.

Yours Respectfully,

MRS. M. A. PIERSON.

Ginger Crisps.

Three pounds of flour, one o sugar, half a pound of butter, same of lard, one pint of molasses, two ounces of ginger, one tablespoon of saleratus.

The following endorsement of the valuable medicinal qualities of Elizir Calisaya or Bark and Iron, is from some of the highest medical authorities in the far west:

A preparation, combining the valuable tonic properties of Calisaya Bark with Iron in an assimilable and tasteless form, has been a desideratum to the profession. We find this skilfully accomplished in a soluble and pleasant form in the "Elixir of Calisaya Bark and Iron" (Pyrophosphate) prepared by our fellow townsman, Mr. B. W. Woodward. The formula and preparation, is one, in our opinion, not to be excelled.

S. B. PRENTISS, M. D. A. M. WILDER, M. D.
J. L. PRENTISS,   " ALBERT NEWMAN, "
M. SUMMERFIELD, " WM. H. SAUNDERS, "
D. SERBER,   " R. MORRIS,   "
S. K. DUSON,   "

Lawrence, June 6th, 1867.

Cocoanut Cake.

One pound of white sugar, half a pound of butter, six eggs, three-qurters of a pound of flour, and one grated cocoanut

Soft Jumbles.

Two cups of sugar, one of butter, one of sour milk, one teaspoon of soda,, two of creamtartar, three eggs, three cups of flour

Rusk

Boil a pint of milk, mix with it while warm, half a cup of lard and butter, and enough white sugar to make them pretty sweet, half a pint of yeast, and enough flour for a pretty stiff batter, grate a nutmeg through, and allow the mixture to stand over night in a warm place—knead flour with them the first thing in the morning, and let them rise again before making out

Aunt Ruth's Cake.

One and a half cups of sugar, one egg, butter the size of an egg, three cups of flour, one cup of milk, half a teaspoon of soda, one of cream-tartar, lemon to taste. Beat the yolk, butter, and sugar together whisk the white light and mix with it, then mix the flour and milk alternately.

Printers, especially those working much at night, are often subject to inflammation of the eyes. E. P Harris, for many years (and still) fore-man of the " Kansas Daily *Tribune*, " was afflicted with a severe inflam-mation of the eyes from over-taxing them in proof-reading—so much so as to be compelled to desist from business. By a timely use of Wood-ward's Kansas Eye Balm, and with only a few applications his eyes were restored to their usual health and vigor. He gives it high praise.

Corn Starch Cake.

One cup of butter, two of sugar, one of corn starch, two of flour, whites of seven eggs, three teaspoons of baking powder. Use the yellows for " one—two—three—four " cakes, with baking powder the same

The following letter from Mrs Judge Goodin is but a sample of hundreds that we might publish, gratefully commending "The Ger-mania "

BALDWIN CITY, April 9th, 1855
Dr Woodward:

Dear Sir: During the last three months my hair has been falling off badly By running my fingers through it, almost a handfull could be taken away. The Germania Hair Renewer was recommended to me and I applied it according to directions The first week I perceived no effect, but on the second it acted like a charm The falling off has entirely stopped and I have used but half a bottle, and, besides, a healthy vigorous growth has commenced, and I consider myself proof against premature baldness. Feeling grateful for the benefit I have derived, I most cheerfully commend it for the purpose designated

C W GOODIN

Molasses Cakes.

Two cups of molasses, on cup of shortening, half cup of boiling water poured on a a teaspoonfull of so la, two table-spoons of ginger, and flour to stiffen soft as you can roll it.

Mrs. W.'s Cookies.

Five cups of flour, two cups of sugar, one cup of butter, two eggs, half a cup of milk, and one teaspoon of soda.

Washington Cake.

One pound of sugar, half a pound of butter, four eggs, one gill of brandy, one gill of sour wine, one gill of sour cream, one teaspoon full of soda, one pound of fruit, one nutmeg—good.

Calisaya, or King's Bark, was unknown to civilization until the middle of the 17th century. Humboldt makes favorable mention of its febrifuge qualities as an antidote to Fever and Ague, Intermittent and Malarious fevers, in his extensive South American travels. The Countess, the wife of the Viceroy of Peru, having experienced the beneficial effects of his Bark, sent it to Europe in 1640. It was sold by the Jesuits for the *normous sum of its own weight in silver*, and was thus called Jesuit's Powder. In 1658, Sir John Talbot employed with great success in France, in the treatment of Fever and Ague, Dyspepsia, Nervous Affections, Loss of Appetite, Weakness and Debility, Palpitation of the Heart, Diarrhea, etc., under the name of English Powders; and in 1679 he sold he secret to Louis the XIV, by whom it was divulged. It is now a standard remedy in all Pharmacopœias, and is employed in the preparation of "Aromatic Elixir Calisaya" and "Elixir of Calisaya Bark and Iron," as manufactured at the laboratory of B. W. Woodward, Proprietor of Woodward's Standard Family Medicines.

Nut Cakes.

One cup of milk, one cup of sugar, one egg, two teaspoonsfull of cream artar, and one of soda stired in the milk, two even teaspoons of melted shortening, and cinnamon—flour to stiffen it.

Apees.

Take half a pound of butter, one pound of flour; half a pound of sugar, a few caraway seeds, a little cinnamon—wet with two eggs, half a glass of water, roll, and cut them out.

Pound Cake.

Mix one pound of sugar with three-quarters pound of butter, when worked white, stir in the yolks of eight eggs beaten to a froth, beat the whole light and stir in—add one pound of sifted flour, mace and nutmeg to taste.

Dr. Woodward's Preparations—"Ague Cure," "Blackberry Syrup," &c., are well known to be the best Remedies of their class

Leroy Pioneer.

California Pudding.

One teacup of suet cut fine, same of molasses and raisins, one cup and a half of sweet milk, four cups of flour, one teaspoon full of soda, and one of salt. Steam three hours, and eat with warm sauce.

Croquets.

Fish or meat intended for croquets must be minced, then placed in a bowl with an equal quantity of crumbs of bread, and seasoned to taste with pepper and salt; after which, according to the quantity of your ingredients, beat up an egg or eggs, whites and yolks together, and mix with the meat and crumbs so as to form a stiff paste; roll into balls about the size of a potato, and fry in melted butter. The fire should not be a fierce one, as croquet, in order to be done thoroughly, should be done slowly. Turn frequently, and fry a light brown.

(From the Kansas State Journal, May 30, 1867.)

Lawrence also promises to become the medicine manufactory and drug emporium of the State. Already the medicines of B. W. Woodward, which have obtained, meritoriously, such great local celebrity, are being ordered by the gross from druggists in St. Louis, Chicago, New York and other Eastern towns. Collins Bros., and other wholesale druggists of St. Louis, have lately ordered a large supply of Woodward's celebrated Blackberry Syrrup. This medicine is justly becoming a great favorite in the West, and only needs to be introduced to become a general favorite with the public. B. W. Woodward also compounds the celebrated Elixir Calisaya Bark and Iron. This medicine is highly recommended by the best physicians of our city and the country generally.

Lemon Ice.

Make a strong lemonade, mix with it the white of eggs beaten very light, and keep stirring all the time it is freezing. Strawberries and other small fruits are very nice when frozen in the same way.

Currant Jelly.

Scald the fruit, squeeze it through a bag, put a pound of sugar to a pint of juice, and boil until it begins to thicken. To preserve currants, take pound for pound; clarify the sugar, add the currants, and boil three-quarters of an hour.

(From the Lawrence Daily Tribune, November 10, 1867.)

With the advent of cool weather, the sickness in the Wakarusa and Kansas Valleys is decreasing, though considerable ague still exists. Dr. B. W. Woodward's Ague Cure, manufactured in this city, is very popular in our localities, and is pronounced, by all who have tried it, to be one of the most effective remedies in use.

Sauce.

Six tablespoons of sugar, two of butter, one egg. Beat well. Add a little boiling water, and wine or nutmeg to the taste.

Cottage Pudding.

One teacup of sugar, one of milk, two and a half tablespoons of melted butter, one egg, one teaspoon of soda, two teaspoons of cream tartar, two teacups of flour. Bake for half an hour in a quick oven.

Swiss Pudding.

Take crumbs of stale bread, with alternate layers of stewed apples (or raw if chopped fine), and a few currants and sugar, with about a quarter of a pound of butter stuck here and there. After this is fixed in your pudding dish' take about a quart of milk, beat five eggs light and mix into the milk, then pour them into your bread. It will take about three-quarters of an hour to bake. Butter and sugar creamed for same.

All Humors of the Blood, Scrofulous habits and Skin Diseases dependent thereon, can be readily removed by the use of Woodward's Blood and Liver Renovator. It is chiefly compounded from NEW REMEDIES, known and used so far only by the *most advanced* of the Medical Profession in this country. Said remedies, as scientifically united in this compound, have an efficacy far transcending that of any of the old-fashioned " Blood Purifiers," " Sarsaparillas," and " Liver Invigorators, inasmuch as this preparation acts directly to eliminate from the fluids all injurious principles, and *Renovates* the tissues of the system. Discard the old and inert compounds and use as remedies only those that are up to the progress of medical science! Use Woodward's Blood and Liver Renovator.

To Prepare Rennet.

Clean and soak in salt water over night, then scrape and stretch on a stick. When dry, cut in small pieces and put one quart of wine to one rennet. Let it stand one week before using.

Rennet Custard.

One tablespoon full of rennet to one quart of milk. Have the milk luke warm and sweetened before the rennet is put in. If you wish it a little yellow, add two eggs.

Tapioca Pudding.

Six tablespoon full of tapioca, one quart of milk, three eggs, sugar and spice to the taste. Heat the milk and tapioca moderately, and bake it one hour.

> "My hair is gray—but not from years,
> Nor grew it white in a single night
> As men's have grown from sudden tears."

If Byron's "Prisoner of Chillon" was living in these progressive times, he could readily, by the use of a very few bottles of Woodward's Germania Hair Renewer, restore his hair to its natural healthful vigor and beautiful color—the same as before he was incarcerated. Such is the improvement in chemical science in this age of the world.

Suet Pudding.

Three cups of flour, one egg, and one cup of suet chopped fine, one cup of sweet milk, one cup of raisins, one teaspoon salt, one cup of molasses, one teaspoon of soda. Put it in a basin and steam three hours. Dressing made with boiling water sweetened and poured on a little butter, with wine or brandy.

Queen of Puddings.

Pour one pint of scalded milk on one of bread crumbs, mix in the yolks of four eggs; bake it half an hour, then take out and put a layer of jelly on the top, then the whites of the eggs beaten light and spread over all, having sweetened both the pudding and the whites first; put all back in the stove long enough to bake the batter a delicate brown—eaten with cream.

" *Comparisons are odorous* "—so says Mrs. Malaprop. Who would pay $1.50 for thirty pills, manufactured " way down East," somewhere, when for *One Dollar*, a bottle of " Woodward's Ague Cure " containing thirty-six pills, can be obtained of any Western Druggist, and far superior to any Eastern Ague pill on the market. These Ague Pills are sold under a guaranty of $5000 that they contain no Arsenic, Strychnia, Mercury, or anything injurious to the system. How is it in this regard with some of the " Tonics " on the market? Speak out, manufacturer! " Under which king, Bezonian?"

Fruit Pudding.

One quart of flour, two teaspoons of cream tartar rubbed in the flour, one teaspoon of soda dissolved in a little milk, salt, and enough milk to make into a stiff dough, roll out thin, and spread a layer of stewed or preserved fruit; roll up together, and put into a cloth, and either steam or boil for one hour and a half—eat with brandy or wine sauce.

" O wad some power the giftie gie us,
    To see oursels as ithers see us,
It wad frae mony a blunder free us
    And foolish notion."

The faculty alluded to by Burns, is undoubtedly a rare one—in fact a great many people are unable to see themselves at all. When they proceed from severe inflammation of the eyelids or eyeballs, use the " Kansas Eye Balm " before going to bed at night, and ten to one, it will " open your eyes " by morning.

Snow-ball Pudding.

One quart of milk, four eggs, beat the whites light, and cook them on the boiling milk; drop it on with a spoon, take off the egg, and stir in the beaten yellows until it makes a custard, adding a little corn starch to make it thick; after taking it off sweeten and flavor the custard, set it away to cool, and put the balls on top when sent to table.

Preserved Citron.

Pare and take the seeds out of your citron, weigh it and put it in a weak brine over night, then boil it in clear water until soft; then take half a pound of sugar to a pound of fruit, make a syrup first, of the sugar and a little of the juice that the fruit has been boiled in, skim it clear and then add the citron; boil it until clear, then take out the fruit and boil the syrup a few minutes longer and skim it, then pour it over the fruit; when cold add a few drops of oil of lemon

German Puffs.

One pint of milk, one pound of flour, two ounces of butter, and four eggs, separate the eggs and beat the yolks until thick, warm the milk, to which add the butter, when cool stir in the yolks, put the flour in a pan and by degrees stir in the above, salt to taste, whisk the whites and stir thorough very lightly. Butter some cups, which half fill with the mixture, and bake in a quick oven. When done, turn them out of the cups and send to table hot. Eat with any kind of sauce preferred.

B. W. WOODWARD's celebrated "Ague Cure" and other remedies have secured him an enviable reputation thoughout Kansas.

Humboldt Union.

Sally Lunn.

Rub three ounces of butter into a pound of flour, then add three eggs beaten very light, a little salt, one gill of yeast, and as much milk as will make it into a soft dough, knead well, and put in a buttered an, cover it and set in a warm place to rise. Bake in a moderate oven, and send to table hot, to be eaten with butter.

Gooseberry Custard.

Stew the berries and put them through a colander, sweeten them and put on the stove again to boil, take off and stir in four eggs well beaten, scald again, and keep stirring. Eat when cold with cream.

DR. WOODWARD with his unrivalled "Ague Cure," can cure all the Chills and Fevers in the West.

Kansas Home Journal.

Lemon Pie.

Two lemons, four eggs, eight tablespoons of white sugar, and two spoonsful of melted butter.

Gelatine.

Pour a quart of cold water on the gelatine, (Cox's is the best), let it stand an hour, then pour on two quarts of boiling water, one pound of crushed sugar, the juice and rinds of two lemons and a tumbler of wine, then strain without heating, stir all in with the hot water.

Corn Fritters.

Grate six ears of corn, three eggs, one tablespoon of flour, a little salt.

Lawrence Lemon Pie.

Two lemons, two cups of sugar, four eggs, one cup of water, eight even teaspoons of flour, butter the size of a walnut, add white of egg lastly. This will make two pies.

Brandy Peaches.

With a sharp knife pare the fruit very thin, weigh it, and allow three-quarters of a pound of sugar to a pound of peaches. Take a part of the sugar and make a thin syrup, scald the fruit and boil it about five minutes only, putting in at a time enough to cover the top of the syrup. As soon as they are done, take them out carefully and spread them on dishes until they are all done. Put the remainder of sugar to the syrup; when it boils set it to cool, and when cold, put a quart of white brandy to each quart of syrup, mix well and put in the fruit. If you wish them very nice, make an entire new syrup.

Mrs. W.'s Lemon Pie.

Two lemons grated; and the inside white cut off close, then squeeze the juice out and chop up the pulp, add two and a half cups of sugar, three eggs broken in three teacups of water, and three tablespoons of corn tarch, wet first in water, stir up the mixture when you pour it into the pan. This makes three pies.

"'Tis sweet to hear the honest watch dog's bark,
Bay deep-mouthed welcome as we draw near home,
'Tis sweet to know there is an eye will mark
Our coming and look brighter when we come."

"Sweet are the uses of adversity," and sweet also, though wholesomely bitter to the taste, is the Aromatic Elixir Calisaya, as prepared by Dr. Woodward. There is no question that this is the best and purest simple tonic and stimulant known.

Green Tomatoe Pie.

Slice the tomatoes, put a layer of them on a paste lined pie-plate, then cover them over with half a teacup of sugar, and part of a lemon, cover with paste; and bake one hour.

Indian Pudding.

Pour enough boiling milk over one quart of corn meal to scald it thoroughly, add a teacup of molasses, three eggs, one teaspoon of ginger and a little salt, then add a little cold milk and a small piece of butter, put in fruit if you wish. Bake in a pudding dish one hour.

Hon C. B. Lines, United States Pension Agent for Kansas, and merchant at Wabaunsee writes, "We shall sell a large quantity of your 'Ague Cure and Blackberry Syrup' this season. No other Ague medicine gives the same satisfaction as yours."

Cookies.

Three and a half pounds of flour, one and a half of sugar, one and a quarter of butter, half a pint of water, one teaspoon of saleratus, mix the flour and butter together, caraway seed to suit the taste

MISCELLANEOUS DISHES.
Stewed Oysters.
Drain the juice from the oysters, and put it on the stove, with milk, a small piece of butter, and pepper and salt to taste, when this comes to a boil add the oysters, and let them remain in just long enough to scald, as it takes away the plumpness and richness of the oyster to cook it too much.

Fried Potatoes.
Pare and cut the potatoes in thin slices, put them in cold water for a few minutes, then dry them in a towel, drop them into very hot fat, enough to float them, the fat from suet is the best, keep turning them until brown on both sides, dip out with a skimmer and salt a little. If properly done, they will be crisp and delicious.

Veal Salad.
Make a mixture of four eggs boiled hard and chopped fine, a bowl full of milk or cream, teaspoon of mustard, with a little vinegar, salt and pepper; Take cold veal, (or any cold meat will do,) chop fine, with a handfull of salad, and then add the other mixture to it.

AROMATIC ELIXIR CALISAYA.—Ladies will find this preparation a nice, delicate cordial and tonic for the weak stomach; and invaluable as a preventive of chills and fever. It is similar in composition to the "Elixir Calisaya Bark and Iron," but contains only the vegetable tonics, without the iron. For sale by all druggists.

French Omelette.
Beat up six eggs with half a pint of cream, or good milk, put in a piece of butter the size of a walnut, and season with pepper and salt; stir all together in a basin or pan, set it on the stove, and as soon as it begins to thicken in the bottom, scrape it loose with a spoon; keep doing this all the time until it is thick all through, but not too stiff. After it once begins to cook it must be kept stirred all the time, or it will stick to the bottom and be tough. It will not take more than a minute to cook all through; pour out in a dish and eat while hot.

How to Keep Hams.
After your hams have taken salt, hang them up and smoke them well, then take them down, and dip them in boiling water for a few seconds; that will kill all the eggs of the insects, if there should be any, then roll them in dry ashes while wet, and hang them up again. Smoke them more if you choose. Those that do their bacon in this way will never have any bugs or skippers on their meat.

Apple Dumplings.
One quart of sour milk, one egg, one teaspoon full of saleratus, one table spoon of lard.

God gives no value unto men
Unmatched with meed of labor,
And cost of worth has ever been
The closest neighbor.
Holland.

Lemon Butter.

Three eggs, three-quarter pounds of sugar, one-quarter pound of butter, three lemons; grate the outside of the lemons, and squeeze the juice out; then mix with it the butter and sugar, and boil; then add the egg, and let boil ten minutes.

Tomatoes for Supper.

For a family of half a dozen persons, take six eggs boil four of them hard, dissolve the yolks with vinegar, add about three teaspoons of mustard, and mash as smooth as possible; then add the two remaining eggs (raw), yolk and white, stir well, then add salad oil, to make altogether sauce sufficent to cover the tomatoes well; add plenty of salt and cayenne pepper, and beat thoroughly until it froots: skin and cut the tomatoes a full fourth of an inch thick, and pour the sauce over

Beckie's Omelet.

Five eggs, one pint of milk, one teaspoon of flour; beat the eggs light, and mix the flour in a little of the milk; then mix it in the egg, with a little salt, and stir in the milk; put a piece of butter the size of a walnut in a pan, and let it get right hot, pour in the omelet, and put it in the stove to bake

Yeast that will not Sour.

Two quarts of water put on to boil, a handfull of hops, tied in a bag, boiled in; also a teacup of brown sugar, and a tablespoon of salt; grate seven potatoes, and boil till it thickens; when nearly cool, add a teacup of yeast

Strawberry Shortcake

Take a quart of flour, a little salt, and make into a dough, with good cream; roll out in one cake, not very thick, bake it; then split it open, butter it and put in the fruit, having previously prepared it by washing and sweetening; then put the two parts together, pour cream over all, and send to table hot

Mother's Sausage.

To twenty pounds of meat, take five tablespoons of salt, three tablespoons of black pepper, and three of sage or pennyroyal.

Scrapple.

Soak a hog's head over night in salt and water; in the morning scrape and cleanse it well, taking out the eyes: then boil it until the meat will drop from the bones: take out and chop fine and return it to the liquor, having previously taken out about one-fourth of it: when it comes to a boil, thicken it with Indian meal to the consistency of mush; season highly with salt and pepper, and whatever herb you wish: boil it about fifteen minutes, stirring constantly that it may not burn; then turn out in a pan, so that when cold it can be cut in slices and fried like mush.

Mince Meat.

Four pounds of beef, boiled until very tender, one pound and a half of suet, two pounds each of sugar, currants and raisins, one and a half ounces of every kind of spice, chop very fine and pack hard in a stone jar: then pour some brandy over the top, or molasses will answer very well. When you wish to use it, to one bowl of the preparation add two or apple, chopped very fine, one-fourth pound of butter, boiled cider, wine, brandy, or other ingredients to your taste.

> "Know how sublime a thing it is
> To suffer and be strong."

It is undoubtedly a "sublime thing" to suffer uncomplainingly; but as far as experience goes, a delicate woman is more apt to grow *weak* than strong under it. It would be much more sensible, after all, to take a bottle of "Elixir Calisaya Bark and Iron," as prepared by Dr. Woodward, and grow "strong" thereby, than to continue to suffer. Thousands of suffering ladies are beginning to find this out, as witness the elastic step, the blooming cheek, and kindling eye, where once was nought but anguished frame and joyless despondency of mind.

Mock Oysters.

Six ears of corn, grated, one egg, a saltspoon of salt, a large spoonfull of sifted flour and a pinch of powdered white sugar, beat up well, and fry in sweet lard—a spoonfull for a cake. Omit the sugar and add some pepper, and the flavor will be like oysters.

Mothers! discard all those vile combinations of laudanum and paregoric, "Soothing Syrups" which drug and stupefy your children. Use for all derangements of the stomach and bowels, Woodward's Aromatic Blackberry Syrup, and you will find its effects healthful and invigorating.

Chicken Pie.

Joint the chicken, and boil until tender, in sufficient water to cover it, season with salt, then line a deep pie-dish with light crust, put the chick n in layers around in the dish, take the liquor it was boiled in, and make a gravy by seasoning with pepper and salt, and a little thickening, pour over the chicken enough to cover it, put a lid of crust over all, with a hole cut in the top to pour more water in if needed. Bake about an hour

Meat Pie

Line the dish as for chicken pie, cut the meat in very small pieces, and cook until tender, then put in a layer of meat, and a layer of oysters (raw), season the liquor and pour over all, put in the top crust and bake it until brown

DR. WOODWARD.--

I have been using your Germania Hair Renewer and wishing to let my friends know the result, you will oblige me by publishing this certificate.

I had used several Hair restoratives before trying yours, but they would not restore the original color.

This has done it perfectly, and my hair is now soft and silky instead of being dry and brash as it was before, and I can truthfully assert that as a Dressing and Restorative it is the finest thing I have ever seen

MRS. F. W. HAMMOND

Fricassee Chickens.

Cut up the chicken and boil in salt water until tender, skim off any scum that arises, and season highly with pepper, salt, and butter, rub a little butter and flour together and thicken the gravy, let it boil up and pour the whole over toasted bread.

Frizzled Beef

Shave down dried beef very thin, and pour hot water over it to freshen it, drain off the water, and frizzle with a little butter, stir in a very little flour until it browns, and last of all add some cream   Let it boil up and it is done.

"Large enough for any man--small enough for any boy." Notwithstanding that Woodward's Aromatic Blackberry Syrup is the gentlest Remedy for all complaints of the Stomach and Bowels with *Children*; it is yet in larger doses the most efficient remedy ever compounded for the severest cases of Diarrhœa and Dysentery of adults. With it you can regulate and control absolutely and safely the morbid action of the Bowels. No case of the cholera has been known where this Remedy was used in time.

Minced Beef.

Boil some fresh beef until tender, pick it to pieces, and season highly with pepper and salt, moisten it a little and tie up in a cloth, and press as you would head cheese. Cut in slices when cold, for tea.

OF THE CHIEF USES OF

WOODWARD'S STANDARD PREPARATIONS.

—o—

Ague and Fever, to cure,   Woodward's Ague Cure
Bad Breath, from Biliary Derangement. Woodward's Blood and Liver
[Renovator.
Bad Breath, from decaying teeth   Woodward's Saponaceous Tooth
[Powder.
Baldness   Woodward's Germania Hair Renewer.
Bath—good in the   Woodward's Crystal Glycerine Soap.
Bitters—the best Tonic..   Woodward's Aromatic Elixir Calisaya.
Bilious Complaints . Woodward's Blood and Liver Renovator.
Boils and Blotches..   "   "   "   "   "
Bowel Complaints   Woodward's Aromatic Blackberry Syrup.
Bronchitis, chronic....Blood and Liver Renovator, (as an Alterative.)
Canker in the Mouth   Blood and Liver Renovator.
Chapped Hands .Crystal Glycerine Soap.
Colic.   Aromatic Blackberry Syrup.
Cholera Infantum.   Aromatic Blackberry Syrup.
Cholera.   as a Preventive—Aromatic Blackberry Syrup.
Complexion, for improving delicacy of   Crystal Glycerine Soap
Costiveness   Blood and Liver Renovator, and Solution Citrate Mag-
[nesia.
Crying and fretting of Infants   Aromatic Blackberry Syrup.
Diarrhœa and Dysentery.   Aromatic Blackberry Syrup
Dyspepsia. good in.   Elixir Calisaya Bark and Iron, and Blood and
[Liver Renovator.
Enlargement of the Bones, Joints, etc   .Blood and Liver Renovator.
Eruptions, on the face or body.. .Blood and Liver Renovator.
Flatulence   Aromatic Blackberry Syrup, and Solution Citrate Mag-
[nesia.
Fevers, Bilious   Ague Cure.
Freckles, for removing....Crystal Glycerine Soap.
Gums, to render hard and healthy....Saponaceous Tooth Powder.
Gray Hair, to restore to natural color.. .Germania Hair Renewer.
Heartburn . Aromatic Blackberry Syrup.
Hypochondria and Hysteria.. .Elixir Calisaya Bark and Iron
Hair, to promote growth of.   Germania Hair Renewer.
  "   for falling off....   "   "   "
  "   for harsh and dry   "   "   "
Hair Dressing, a perfect... Woodward's Fragrant Oil of Sunflowers.
Impurity of the Blood.. . Blood and Liver Renovator.
Jaundice...   "   "   "   "
King's Evil, or Scrofula.   "   "   "   "
Liver Complaints   "   "   "   "

Loss of Appetite   Aromatic Elixir Calisaya.
Lowness of Spirits   Elixir Calisaya Bark and Iron.
Mania or Melancholy   Elixir Calisaya Bark and Iron, and Blood and
                                              [Liver Renovator.
Nursery, for use in the   Crystal Glycerine Soap, and Aromatic Black
                                              [berry Syrup.
Nervousness   Elixir Calisaya Bark and Iron.
Neuralgia   Elixir Calisaya Bark and Iron, and Ague Cure.
Pains in the Head and Back.   Blood and Liver Renovator.
Pains in the Stomach and Bowels   Aromatic Blackberry Syrup.
Pimples and Pustules   Blood and Liver Renovator.
Piles   "   "   "   "
Preventive of Chills and Fevers   Aromatic Elixir Calisaya.
Salt Rheum or Tetter   Blood and Liver Renovator.
Scrofula   "   "   "   "
Scalp, for irritations of the   Germania Hair Renewer.
Sick and Nervous Headache   Blood and Liver Renovator, and Elixir
                                              [Calisaya Bark and Iron.
Sore Eyes   Woodward's Kansas Eye Balm.
Sore Mouth   Blood and Liver Renovator.
Shaving, during or after, use   Crystal Glycerine Soap.
Skin Diseases   Blood and Liver Renovator, and Crystal Glycerine Soap.
Summer Complaint   Aromatic Blackberry Syrup.
Sunburn, good for   Crystal Glycerine Soap.
Tan, to remove   "   "   "
Teeth, to prevent decay of   Saponaceous Tooth Powder.
Teething Children, to quiet   Aromatic Blackberry Syrup.
Tonic—as a general invigorator   Aromatic Elixir Calisaya.
Urinary Diseases   Blood and Liver Renovator.
Weakness of the Eyes   Kansas Eye Balm.

From the Topeka Leader, Dec. 4, 1867.

One of the most enterprising men in the State of Kansas is Mr. B. W. Woodward, of Lawrence. Locating in that city in the year 1855, he is now one of the oldest settlers in the State. Since that time, notwithstanding many reverses, he has become very successful in the Drug business; and he has compounded several Medicines that have gained for him a good name wherever they have been introduced.

___

Woodward's Compound Aromatic Blackberry Syrup is a healthful, pleasant and efficient remedy for Diarrhœa, Dysentery, Colic, Cholera, Summer Complaint, Cholera Morbus, and all deranged conditions of the Stomach and Bowels. It is specially suitable for Children while teething, to correct the Stomach and Bowels.

Woodward Ague Cure cures effectually, restoring tone and vigor to the system.

Currant Wine.

Press the juice from the fruit, and to a pint of juice put a pound of sugar and a quart of water, let this stand until it ferments, then rack it off and bottle for use—fit for use in six weeks.

Blackberry Wine.

Measure the berries and bruise them, to every gallon adding one quart of boiling water, let the mixture stand twenty-four hours, stirring occasionally, then strain off the liquor into a cask, to every gallon adding two pounds of sugar; cork tight and let stand until the following October, and you will have wine ready for use.

"Night is the time for rest—
How sweet when labors close
To draw around an aching breast
The curtain of repose—
Stretch the tired limbs and lay the head
Upon our own delightful bed."

But how can you rest when suffering "young hopeful," undergoing the severe ordeal of his "teething time," disturbs the quiet of your peaceful slumbers by his cries of pain? Simply by administering a portion of Woodward's Aromatic Blackberry Syrup. It allays all irritation, cures Diarrhea and Dysentery and corrects all irregularities of the Stomach and Bowels to which children are especially liable during that disturbing season. "So shall your days be tranquil and your nights happy." Selah!

Raspberry Vinegar.

Red raspberries, any quantity, or sufficient to fill a stone jar nearly full, then pour upon them sufficient vinegar to cover them. Cover the jar closely, and set it aside for eight or ten days, then strain through flannel or muslin, and add to the clear liquor one and a half pounds of sugar to each pint, place over the fire and boil gently for a few minutes, then allow it to cool, and bottle for use. This makes, when mixed with water, a delightful summer drink.

Cream Nectar.

Three pounds of loaf sugar, one quart of water, two ounces of tartaric acid; when boiling hot add the whites of two eggs, boil five minutes, then skim off the top, then cool and bottle it ; flavor with anything you choose. Two tablespoonsful of the cream and a small quantity of soda to a glass of water.

Soothing and grateful to the inflamed lid or ball—a very few applications of the "Kansas Eye Balm" will relieve the sorest eyes. Try it.

Currant Shrub.

To every pint of juice add half a pound of sugar, boil it well, but slowly and skim; when cold add to every pint half a gill of brandy and bottle it.

The following is from Prof. T J. Cook, late of New York City, and author of the "Olive Branch," "Union," "New Olive Branch," and other musical works:

Dr. B. W. Woodward: After an extended trial of the medicinal properties of the "Elixir of Calisaya Bark and Iron," as prepared by you, I can state that, as a nervous stimulant, a most pleasant and palatable tonic, and as a general invigorator to the system, when debilitated, I have found it most beneficial indeed.   T J. Cook.

Hundreds of testimonials similar to the following might be given.

B W. Woodward:

Sir: Having for the past three years used your Blackberry Syrup in our families, we take great pleasure in recommending it to the public. In several severe cases of diarrhea and dysentery, we have found it always efficient—never failing to give relief immediately. It is happily adapted to the troubles of children in teething ; and, altogether, we would not dispense with it in our families upon any account
                W. H Fisher, Ag't Northwestern Life Ins Co.
                Jos Hemphill, Ag't N Y Nat Life Ins. Co
                Bob Wilson, Deitzler Vineyard Nurseries
Lawrence, Kansas, May 14, 1867

Dr. B W. Woodward:

Dear Sir: Having suffered very much for the past year from Indigestion and General Debility, and for the past three months with Chills and Fever, I was induced to use your "Ague Cure," and "Calisaya Bark and Iron," having tried several different remedies without any apparent good effect.
    Your "Ague Cure" has cured me of the Chills; and, after taking two bottles of your " Bark and Iron," I am enabled to eat my regular meals without distress of stomach following, which had not been the case for nearly a year, or until I commenced taking your preparation. I cheerfully recommend it to all who are similarly affected
                J D. Whitten

Mr Whitten is of the firm of Fuekler & Whitten, General Agents for the State of Kansas for the well known Connecticut Mutual Life Insurance Company

From the Kansas Daily Tribune.

It is a subject of remark that the "untimely frosts of age" on hair and beard of our citizens are fast disappearing, and "raven locks and tresses" are again asserting their sway. The injurious Hair Dyes are now discarded, as the "Germania Hair Renewer" restores the *life* with the *color* of the hair. A guaranty of $1000 is offered by the proprietor that it contains neither Nitrate of Silver nor Sugar of Lead, found in so many of the Hair Restoratives of the day.

Reliable Medicines.

Amid the variety of Proprietary Medicines that spring up from time to time, there is occasionally one of sterling merit that obtains a hold upon the popular confidence, and becomes, as it were, a household necessity. Such is, emphatically, the case with the preparations of the great Lawrence Druggist, B. W. Woodward. His "Ague Cure" has now been before the public for several years, and the best evidence of its worth is the increasing demand for it. The cure of ague is something about which people cannot be humbugged. If a man has "the chills," he will know it, and he will know when he is relieved of them. Woodward's Ague Cure is just what it claims to be; and so effective is it that the demand for it has become quite general throughout the West, and is every day on the increase.

We might make the same remarks of Woodward's Blackberry Syrup, one of the best medicines for those diseases of the bowels which prevail throughout the West that we have ever known.—*Lawrence Republican.*

A DESERVED COMPLIMENT.—The Manhattan *Independent* pays the following deserved compliment to our townsman, Mr. B. W. Woodward, and his celebrated medicines:

"We are pleased to learn that this eminent druggist, of Lawrence, Kansas, has been extending his business and the sale of his valuable remedies into other and distant States. Large orders have been received and filled of late, from wholesale houses in Cleveland, Chicago and other distant cities. However these valuable medicines may be esteemed abroad, we can hardly suppose the estimation in which they are held in other States will exceed their popularity at home. We are happy to testify from personal knowledge to the efficacy of at least one of his preparations.

ALL OF
Woodward's Standard Preparations,
TOILET AND MEDICINAL,
FOR SALE BY

www.ingramcontent.com/pod-product-compliance
Lightning Source LLC
Chambersburg PA
CBHW021605270326
41931CB00009B/1371